D0811848

DISCARD

Date: 6/7/16

J 621.8 WEA
Weakland, Mark,
Fred Flintstone's adventures
with screws : righty tighty,

PALM BEACH COUNTY
LIBRARY SYSTEM
3650 SUMMIT BLVD.
WEST PALM BEACH, FL 33406

FRED FLINTSTONE'S ADVENTURES with SCREWS

Righty Tighty, Lefty Loosey

by Mark Weakland
illustrated by Loic Billiau

CAPSTONE PRESS
a capstone imprint

A screw is closely related to an inclined plane. They both have a slanted surface. But a screw's slanted surface turns in a spiral. So a screw, like this spiral staircase, is really an inclined plane spiraling around a post.

Some screws hold things together. Others lift or lower materials. The staircase is an example of a screw that helps things move from a high place to a low place. It's how Dino got from upstairs to downstairs. Breakfast time, boy! With a screw, things can be moved with less effort and in smaller spaces.

A slide can be a screw.
Sliding around and around is fun!

Like the staircase and kitchen stool, Bamm-Bamm's toy is an example of a screw. The spiral helps a rolling marble move from a high place to a low place. As the marble rolls, it travels downward along a slanted inclined plane. Wilma, I'm heading outside!

Sure, Fred.

A steel screw on a jack isn't very big, but it can lift a lot of weight.

A cider press crushes fruit into juice.

Yum, yum!

Now it's time to get back to work, Barney! This drill uses a screw. The part that digs into the wood has a twisting inclined plane. In this way it is like a spiral staircase. But the edge of the inclined plane is sharp. The sharp edge allows the drill to tunnel into all types of materials.

A drill bit looks like a spiral staircase. Both are examples of screws.

This screw will hold two pieces of wood together.

Threads

Plastic water bottles and pop bottles use screws.

Sure, honey, I can help. Bottles, jars, and their caps or lids have threads. The threads are screws that hold the cap or lid tightly in place.

19

Glossary

drill—to make a hole

force—a push or pull exerted upon an object

inclined plane—a slanting surface that is used to move objects to different levels

materials—the substances from which something is made

nut—a small metal piece with a hole in the middle that screws on to a bolt and holds it in place

press—a device for applying pressure to something in order to flatten it or to make juice or oil

rotate—to spin around

spiral—a pattern that goes around in circles; the spiral on a screw is an inclined plane

thread—the raised, spiral ridge around a screw; a thread is also the raised, spiral ridge around a bottle or jar and its cap or lid

Read More

LaMachia, Dawn. *Screws at Work.* Zoom in on Simple Machines. New York: Enslow Publishing, 2016.

Miller, Jerry. Screws. *Simple Machine Science.* New York: Gareth Stevens Pub., 2013.

Oxlade, Chris. *Making Machines with Screws.* Simple Machine Projects. Chicago: Heinemann Raintree, 2015.

Internet Sites

FactHound offers a safe, fun way to find Internet sites related to this book. All of the sites on FactHound have been researched by our staff.

Here's all you do:

Visit *www.facthound.com*

Type in this code: 9781491484784

 Super-cool stuff!

Check out projects, games and lots more at
www.capstonekids.com

Index

Look for all the books in the series:

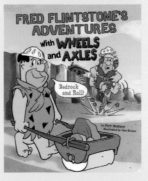

Thanks to our adviser for his expertise, research, and advice:
Paul Ohmann, PhD, Associate Professor of Physics
University of St. Thomas, St. Paul, Minnesota

Published in 2016 by Capstone Press, A Capstone Imprint
1710 Roe Crest Drive, North Mankato, Minnesota 56003
www.mycapstone.com

Copyright © 2016 Hanna-Barbera.
FLINTSTONES and all related characters and elements are
trademarks of and © Hanna-Barbera.
WB SHIELD: ™ & © Warner Bros. Entertainment Inc.
(s16) CAPS35040

All rights reserved. No part of this publication may be
reproduced in whole or in part, or stored in a retrieval system,
or transmitted in any form or by any means, electronic,
mechanical, photocopying, recording, or otherwise, without
written permission of the publisher.

Library of Congress Cataloging-in-Publication Data
Weakland, Mark, author.
  Fred Flintstone's adventures with screws : righty-tighty, lefty-
loosey / by Mark Weakland ; illustrated by Loic Billiau.
  pages cm — (Flintstones explain simple machines)
Summary: "Popular cartoon character Fred Flintstone explains
how screws work and how he uses simple machines in his daily
life"—Provided by publisher
Audience: 6–8.
Audience: K to grade 3.
ISBN 978-1-4914-8478-4 (library binding)
ISBN 978-1-4914-8484-5 (eBook PDF)
1. Screws—Juvenile literature. 2. Simple machines—
Juvenile literature. I. Billiau, Loic, illustrator. II. Title. III.
Title: Adventures with screws. IV. Series: Weakland, Mark.
Flintstones explain simple machines.
TJ1338.W43 2016
621.8'82—dc23   2015024735

Editorial Credits
Editor: Alesha Halvorson
Designer: Ashlee Suker
Creative Director: Nathan Gassman
Media Researcher: Tracy Cummins
Production Specialist: Kathy McColley

The illustrations in this book were created digitally.

Image Credits
Shutterstock: Firma V, 13, megastocker, 19, Nagy-Bagoly
Arpad, 14, Neale Cousland, 9, rukawajung, 10, Vivid Pixels, 17

Printed in the United States of America in
North Mankato, MN. 092015 009221CGS16